KU-450-966

I WAS THERE

ANCIENT GREECE

JOHN D. CLARE

Consultant Editor MICHAEL EDWARDS

THE BODLEY HEAD
LONDON

First published in Great Britain in 1993
by The Bodley Head Children's Books
Random House UK Limited
20 Vauxhall Bridge Road, London SW1V 2SA

Random House Australia (Pty) Limited
20 Alfred Street, Sydney, NSW 2061, Australia

Random House New Zealand Limited
18 Poland Road, Glenfield, Auckland 10, New Zealand

Random House South Africa (Pty) Limited
PO Box 337, Bergvlei 2012, South Africa

Copyright © 1993 Random House UK Limited
Photographs © 1993 Charles Best

The right of Random House UK Limited to be identified
as the originator of this work has been asserted by the
company in accordance with the Copyright, Designs and
Patents Act, 1988.

All rights reserved

ISBN 0-370-31834-X

A CIP catalogue record for this book is available from
the British Library.

Director of Photography Tymn Lintell
Photography Charles Best
Production Manager, Photography Fiona Nicholson
Designer Dalia Hartman
Visualizer Antony Parks
Editor Gilly Abrahams
Series Editor Helen Wire
Research Sheila Smith
Maps and time-line John Laing
Map and time-line illustrations David Wire
Jacket concept Peter Bennett
Typeset 11/14 Palatino Sue Estermann
Reproduction Scantrans, Singapore

Printed and bound in China

ACKNOWLEDGEMENTS

Casting: Baba's Crew (UK), Jenny Panoutsopoulou (Greece).
Costumes: Val Metheringham, Angi Woodcock. Locations,
Greece: Susan Pugh-Tasios, Pat Arvaniti. Make-up: Emma Scott.
Props: Cluny South, Marisa Rossi. Runners: Zoë Pagnamenta
(Greece and UK); Catherine Stroobants (Greece). Sets and
transport: Road Runner Film Services and Peter Knight.

Random House Children's Books would also like to thank:
Roger Tonks, Angels; The Benaki Foundation, Athens; Peter
G. Calligas, Acropolis Museum, Athens; Chislehurst Caves;
The Corporation of London for Hill House, Hampstead; Lady
Eleni Cubitt; Nick Fields, British School, Athens; Mr Digby,
Flame Enterprises; Mrs Cornelia Hajiaslani, First Ephorate of
Prehistoric and Classical Antiquities; Red Saunders, Four Walls
Studio; Greca International Transports; Commander Stavros
Platis, Hellenic Navy Base, Piraeus; the staff, Joint Library of
the Hellenic and Roman Societies; Saridis Furniture Show-
room, Athens; Scene Dock; Mr Petts, Spink & Son Ltd; Douli
Thanopoulou; Mr Tiriopoulos, Zappeion Conference Centre;
Kyrios Vangelis; and special thanks to Mr Tim Angel.

Additional photographs: American School of Classical Studies
at Athens: Agora Excavations, p27 bottom left, p63 left. Ancient
Art & Architecture Collection, p10, p16 middle left, top right.
Ashmolean Museum, p45 middle, p51 top right. Bildarchiv
Preussischer Kulturbesitz, Berlin, p21. British Museum, p6 left,
p16 bottom left, p27 top and right, p41 top, p45 left and right.
Ecole Française d'Archéologie, Athens, p63 top. Kevin Fleming/
Ulysses Archive, pp18-19. Hellenic Navy, pp28-29. Michael Hol-
ford, p11, p12, p14, p52, p57, p62 left and bottom. Metropolitan
Museum of Art: Fletcher Fund, 1932 (32.11.1), photograph
Schecter Lee, p30 left; Rogers Fund, 1914 (14.130.12) p17.
Museum of Fine Arts, Boston, H.L. Pierce Fund, p9. Luciano
Pedicini, p28, p35, pp54-55. Royal Ontario Museum, Toronto,
p13, p31 bottom. Scala, p6 right, p7, p31 top. Staatlichen
Antikensammlungen und Glyptothek, Munich, photograph
Studio Koppermann, p30 bottom.

Contents

The Greek World

The philosopher Socrates (*c.* 470-399 BC) lived in Athens in ancient Greece. Although he was described as 'the wisest man of his time', he knew nothing of America, or electricity, or germs. In the morning, he needed only to dress simply in his sheet before walking to the market-place.

In many ways, ancient Greek society may seem primitive and unsophisticated to us. Yet in the centuries after 500 BC, Greek ideas dominated and changed the world. Two thousand five hundred years later, much of western government and culture is still influenced by the ancient Greek ways of thinking and living.

Many modern states are democracies and believe in the principle of rule 'by the people, for the people'. The Greeks developed this idea of government (see page 26). The word democracy comes from two Greek words: *demos* (people) and *kratos* (power).

Perhaps more importantly, the Greeks developed a way of thinking called philosophy.
They actively tried to understand things. The Greek word *philosophos* means a man who likes to be wise. Many modern proverbs come from ancient Greece. For instance, the Greek saying: 'Like to like, jackdaw to jackdaw', was translated in 1578 by an English writer as 'Byrds of a fether, best flye together'. The word 'idea' is a Greek word. Greek ideas are the foundation of modern thinking about science and medicine, mathematics and geography.

The design of many houses and public buildings owes much to Greek architecture.

The Greeks invented competitive sport. The modern Olympic Games are based on the games held every four years at Olympia in southern Greece. Words such as athletics, stadium and marathon all come from the Greek language.

The Greeks also invented drama. Words such as theatre, comedy and tragedy come from the Greek.

The First Greeks

Nobody really knows where the Greeks came from. Historians think they developed from a number of different tribes from India and central Europe. The historian Martin Bernal, however, in a book called *Black Athena*, has claimed they came from Egypt and Africa.

The Greeks were not the first civilized people. On Crete, a large island south of mainland Greece, archaeologists have found the ruins of rich palaces dating from about 2000 BC. They belonged to a people called the Minoans. In about 1600 BC a similar civilization developed at Mycenae on the mainland of Greece. It used a kind of writing which historians call 'Linear B'. Writing, however, had been known in the Middle East since before 3000 BC, and the first cities date from a thousand years earlier than that.

Mycenae was destroyed in about 1200 BC. Historians think that the next four hundred years were a Dark Age of wars, invasions and movements of tribes. Then, after 800 BC, Greek civilization began to develop. Iron-making became common. The Greeks learned to write using a Syrian alphabet. They began to make beautiful, decorated pots. The population started to increase.

The City-States

The Greeks thought of themselves as one people, the Hellenes (it was the Romans who called them Greeks). They despised most foreigners, calling them barbarians (because foreign languages sounded like a ridiculous 'bar-bar' to Greek ears).

Greece, however, was never a united country in ancient times. The mainland is divided by rocky mountain ranges. Southern Greece is almost completely cut off from the north by the Gulf of Corinth. In the Aegean Sea there are many small islands. Ancient Greece, therefore, was divided into dozens of tiny states, each comprising a city and the nearby farmland. Athens was by far the largest. Corinth, Thebes and Sparta were also important, but the rest were much smaller. The city-states continually fought each other.

Each city-state was ruled in a different way. Our word politics comes from the Greek

word *polis*, meaning city. Some were democracies. In others, a tyrant seized power and ruled by himself. Sparta, unlike any other *polis*, was governed by two kings, who were advised by a council of men over 60 years old. Most city-states, however, were controlled by a small group of rich landowners and noblemen. The modern word aristocrat comes from the Greek words *aristos* (the best) and *kratos* (power). It was believed that the aristocrats were the best qualified people to make the decisions.

After about 593 BC, the people of the city of Athens decided that their society had four classes, all of which owned land. At the top were the *pentakosiomedimnoi*, the richest nobles. Next came the *hippeis*, rich enough to own horses (*hippoi*). Below them were the *zeugitai*, men with a plough and two oxen, and the *thetes*, the poorest landowners.

Even the *thetes*, they believed, were superior to women, and to the *metoikoi* (Greeks from other city-states, living in Athens). The women and the *metoikoi* were not allowed to vote or own land and were not regarded as citizens. The philosopher Plato gave thanks 'first that he was a human being rather than an animal; second that he was a man rather than a woman; then that he was a Greek and not a foreigner; and finally that he lived in Athens'.

Aspects of ancient Greek civilization: far left, a statuette of the philosopher Socrates; left, two theatre masks (see page 32); and, above, a Greek warrior under attack.

Farming in Attica

Athens, the largest city-state in Greece, was about the size of present-day Luxembourg. In 431 BC it had a population of perhaps a quarter of a million people. The countryside around Athens, which had to provide food for the Athenians, was called Attica. It was hilly and the soil was shallow and rocky. There was little rain. Plato wrote that Attica was like 'the skeleton of a body withered by disease – the soil has fallen away, leaving the land all skin and bone'.

Farming, therefore, was hard work. In winter the cold north winds would 'skin an ox', and in summer 'the sun scorches head and knees', wrote Hesiod, a Greek farmer and poet who lived in the eighth century BC. Wealthy estate-owners, who had slaves, horses and oxen to do the work, could afford large farmhouses and town houses. The poor peasants, however, had 'for robe but a rag, for bed just a bag of rushes – the home of a nation of bugs whose fierce and tireless bites keep you awake at night. And then for carpet a sodden old mat, and a hard stone for a pillow, and a broken barrel for a chair'.

Townspeople joked that country people were slow and stupid. Asked if he is a farmer, a character in one Greek comedy replies angrily: 'Do I *look* like an idiot?' However, the

majority of Greeks worked on the land, producing the food on which the townspeople depended. And after the harvest, wrote Hesiod, country life was wonderful, 'when the grasshopper sings, and the goats are fattest and the women most beautiful…then I'll have a shady rock and bright wine, a bowl of curds, some goat's milk and a nice piece of veal'.

A farmer loads his donkey. He is taking his produce – eggs, chickens, cheese and vegetables – to sell in the market-place in Athens (see page 49). His daughters make bread while his son milks the goat – cows' milk is thought to be too rich for Greek stomachs. Against the farmhouse wall rest the sickles they use to reap the barley crop, and (behind the farmer) a plough. From the branches of the olive trees, cheeses hang in linen bags to strain out the whey (water).

Athenian farmers grow mainly olives, which do well even without much rain. Above: a man is adding his weight to that of a bag of rocks on the press to help squeeze out the oil. Olive oil is used for cooking, to provide lamplight and to remove dirt from the body.

Sparta

Sparta, for a long time the most powerful Greek city-state, was unique in every way.

The Spartans forced the inhabitants of neighbouring areas, whom they had en-slaved, to do all their farming and trading for them. Their only aim in life was to be a nation of fierce warriors. The Spartan army was believed to be unbeatable. Unlike other city-states, Sparta had no walls; its soldiers were thought to be protection enough.

Spartan children belonged to the state, not to their parents. The elders inspected all new-born babies; those that were sickly or weak were left on the hills to die.

Until the age of seven, a boy lived with his mother. This did not mean he was pampered. Spartan women sent their husbands off to war with the words: 'Come back with your shield – or [dead] on it.' A Spartan mother might kill her son if he was a coward.

At seven, Spartan boys went to live in army barracks to be trained by a *paidonomos* (child-ruler). They had no other education.

Spartan men always ate together in their barracks, so that everyone could see if anyone was eating or drinking too much. The young

men ate in silence, lowering their eyes as a mark of respect for their elders. Their meals usually consisted of barley bread, fruit, cheese and a revolting black broth. 'Now I understand why Spartans do not fear death,' remarked one visitor.

Although a young man usually married at 20, he had to live ten more years in the barracks, slipping away secretly at night to visit his wife. It was not uncommon for a young Spartan woman to give birth to the baby of a man she had rarely seen in daylight.

Spartan men were not allowed to show pain or weakness. In one story a youth, who had stolen a fox and hidden it in his shirt, was stopped on his way back to the barracks by an older man. Spartan children had to show respect for their elders, so the boy talked to the man, ignoring the fox which was biting his chest and stomach. When he returned to the barracks he died of his wounds – but he had not flinched.

Left: Spartan girls are trained in athletics, so they will grow strong and bear strong children; they wear so little that Greeks from other city-states are shocked.

Above: Spartan men boxing; they wear *himantes* – gloves made of ox-hide thongs tied around their hands.

Below: Spartan boys have no shoes and wear only a thin tunic, even in winter. They are encouraged to steal food but are whipped if they are caught.

Gods and Heroes

The Greeks worshipped many gods. The gods were said to live on Mount Olympus, in northern Greece. The Greeks believed that the gods were immortal (would never die).

Zeus, the king of the gods, was the god of thunder and lightning, gold and kings. His son, Apollo, the god of light and purity, was the lord of music, healing and guidance. Athene, the goddess of Athens, was the goddess of war, handicrafts and wisdom. Demeter was the goddess of harvest and Aphrodite was the goddess of love. Other immortals were Dionysus the god of wine, acting and destruction; Poseidon, god of the sea; and Hades, lord of the dead.

The Greeks had many myths (stories) about their gods. These stories are full of violence and cruelty. In one myth, the god Cronos (Time) cuts his father into pieces and swallows his own children whole. Another legend is about Typhon, a fierce monster with dragon's wings and a hundred heads, each mouth roaring, howling and shouting in a different voice. Zeus defeated Typhon by throwing the island of Sicily on top of him, where he lay, struggling to free himself.

Many of these stories are clearly attempts to answer questions about things the ancient Greeks did not have enough scientific knowledge to explain. The story of Typhon, for instance, explained for the Greeks the volcanic eruptions of Mount Etna in Sicily.

Where do we come from? The myths said that the god Prometheus made man from clay. Where did fire come from? Prometheus stole fire from Zeus and gave it to man. In this myth, to punish Prometheus, Zeus tied him to a rock. Each day an eagle came and ate his liver, which grew whole again overnight.

The Greeks believed that the gods were powerful, but also that they were cruel, jealous troublemakers. This explained pain,

disease and disaster. According to one story, when the gods gave Athens to Athene, Poseidon was so angry that he sent a huge tidal wave to flood the land.

Historians think that such stories are folk memories of actual events. Geologists have found evidence of a huge volcanic eruption on the Mediterranean island of Santorini in about 1500 BC, which would have caused a tidal wave.

The Heroes

Greek stories about human heroes may also be based on actual events in the distant past. In one story the hero, Heracles of Thebes, completes a number of labours (tasks), including overcoming animals such as the enormous lion of Nemea and the bull of Minos. Perhaps there was once a ruler of Thebes who was a skilled hunter, or who defeated those states.

Theseus, another hero, killed the Minotaur (a monster with the head of a bull and the body of a man) and became the ruler of Athens. Historians think this story mixes folk memories of human sacrifices to bulls in Minoan Crete with stories of a successful king of Athens during the Dark Age.

The *Iliad* is a long poem written by the Greek poet Homer. It tells the story of a war against the city of Troy in Asia Minor. It may describe actual raids on the city by Greek pirates; archaeologists have found evidence that Troy was attacked and burned a number of times.

The Athenians believe that 'grey-eyed Athene', the goddess of Athens, gave olives and women to men. It is said that she was born when Hephaistos, the blacksmith god, split open the head of Zeus with an axe (left).

Right: the statue of Athene in the Parthenon temple in Athens is 12 metres (40 feet) high and plated with gold.

Sacrifice and Superstition

The Greeks believed that, although the gods were far off and remote, their blessing or curse could bring instant success or disaster. Many people, therefore, were very superstitious. If a cat ran in front of them, they refused to move until they had thrown three stones across the road. If they heard an owl hoot, they shouted: 'Athene is queen!'

The best way to please the gods was to offer sacrifices, usually a sheep or a pig. First, they threw barley over the animal, then they slit its throat, burned the thigh-bones and finally cooked and ate the rest of the meat. Such a ceremony was common in Greek families, and poor people clubbed together to buy an animal between them. Everybody joined in, laying their hands on the animal, while the head of the household prayed to the gods for health and wealth. He prayed standing up, with his arms raised. The prayer of Socrates was: 'Dear gods of this place, grant me to be beautiful within.'

Religion was a public affair. All the inhabitants of Athens took part in the festival of *Panathenaea* (the Greek word *pan* means 'all'). 'Athene, our city's protector, queen of a land, powerful in war, come to us bringing victory,' the people sang as they marched through the city.

Most festivals were farming ceremonies. At *Thargelia*, the festival of the first fruits, boys hung branches on the front doors of their houses. During *Anthesteria*, the festival of Dionysus, the god of wine, men got drunk in total silence, then shouted: 'Get out, Spirits of the Dead.' The festival of the Eleusinian Mysteries – held in late summer in honour of Demeter, the goddess of harvest – lasted 21 days and finished with a 14-mile (23-kilometre) walk from Athens to Eleusis.

The Greeks believed that the gods watched these festivals. To amuse them, they put on athletics contests and races in which the runners carried burning torches, as well as competitions between actors, speakers and choirs.

Left: this vase painting shows the goddess Demeter sending a messenger to Greece with the gift of corn.

Right: there are about 250 oracles in Greece. The Oracle of Apollo at Delphi is the most famous. People go there to seek the god's advice before embarking on a new venture. They wash themselves and sacrifice an animal, then they go into the Adyton, the most holy place. Beneath the Adyton is a cavern through which a stream flows. A priestess called the Pythoness breathes in fumes from the stream and chews laurel leaves until she is in a drugged frenzy. Her screams and ravings are thought to be a message from Apollo. A priest listens to her, then interprets the message for the visitors, often in the form of a riddle.

The Olympic Games

The Olympic Games were held in honour of Zeus, at Olympia in southern Greece. The first games took place in 776 BC. They were held every four years and became a major religious festival. People from all over Greece took part. 'The games bring us together and create peace and understanding among us,' said the orator (speaker) Lysias in 388 BC.

The five-day festival was held in summer. There was a month-long sacred truce, during which war between the city-states stopped, so that the twenty thousand priests, competitors and spectators were able to travel to the games. Most visitors slept in tents, but in later times important guests stayed in a huge building called the Leonidaion. A large

marble temple was also built. It contained a huge gold and ivory statue of Zeus, which came to be known as one of the seven wonders of the ancient world.

The festival started with prayers and religious ceremonies, then the games began. Competitions included horse racing, boxing and a *pentathlon* of five events: a 180-metre (200-yard) sprint race, throwing the javelin and discus, long jumping and wrestling. In another wrestling competition called the *pankration*, the fighters were allowed to do anything apart from biting or gouging out an opponent's eye. The judge carried a stick and hit anybody who cheated. There were also competitions in public speaking and poetry.

Winners at Olympia became celebrities. In 415 BC one Athenian, Alcibiades, was appointed as general of a military expedition just because he had entered seven chariots in one race and had taken first, second and fourth places. In Sparta, Olympic winners had the honour of fighting in the front rank in the next war.

Right: ancient Greeks are not embarrassed by nudity. The athletes shown on this amphora (pot) from about 530 BC are competing naked, as are the riders in the horse race, below left.

Above: a carving on the base of a statue. Two athletes are wrestling, and a javelin-thrower tests the point of his javelin. To the left is an athlete in the usual starting position for a race. The sprint race takes place on the third day of the Games, when an ox is sacrificed to Zeus and the winner is allowed to set fire to the sacrifice.

Above left: every athlete longs for the victor's ribbon. Although his prize is a simple laurel wreath, when he returns home he will be loaded with presents, freed from paying taxes, or given free meals for the rest of his life.

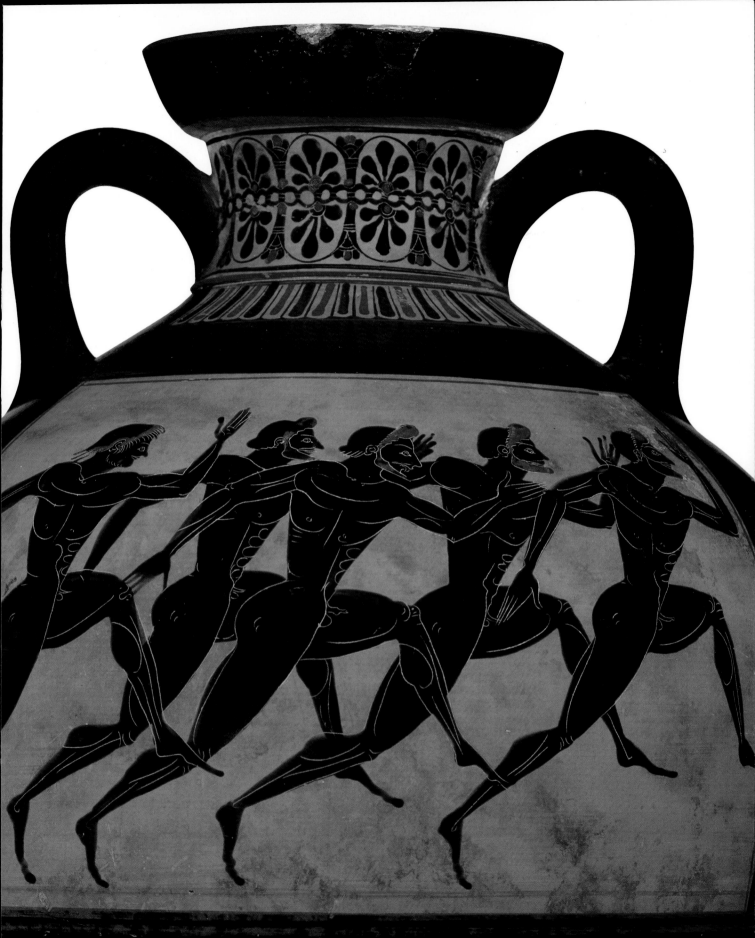

The Greek Colonies

 At about the same time that the Greeks started holding the Olympic Games, Greek civilization began to develop in other ways. One feature of this was that Greeks sailed to other countries to set up new city-states, called 'colonies'.

They went for many reasons. Sometimes they were asked to leave, usually when the population of their city had outgrown the amount of food that could be produced on the surrounding farmland. In such cases, a respected local man was appointed as 'founder', to lead the expedition. Sometimes a section of the population that was being badly treated would emigrate, hoping to find a better life. It was not unknown for a whole city, at war with a powerful neighbour, to pack up and sail away to a safer place.

The first colonies were set up in Sicily, Italy and Asia Minor (present-day Turkey). Later settlements were established as far apart as Massilia (Marseilles) in southern France, Naucratis in Egypt, and Olbia (near the Crimea) on the Black Sea. One historian has estimated that there were 150 city-states in Greece, but 1,500 colonies all around the Mediterranean and the Black Sea. Most colonies were copies of the Greek city-states and many became centres of Greek civilization and learning.

This colonization continued for eight centuries. After the conquests of Alexander the Great (see page 57), settlements were set up in Persia, Afghanistan and the Punjab and on the coasts of southern India, spreading Greek culture all over the known world.

Greek colonists on a merchant ship. The map shows the main Greek settlements around the Mediterranean and the Black Sea in about 500 BC.

Marathon

The spread of Greek colonies around the Mediterranean and Black Sea brought Greece to the attention of the great Persian Empire which was growing in the Middle East (see map). In 492 BC the Persian king, Darius I, sent ambassadors to the Greeks, demanding that they accept him as their master. The Athenians' reply was to throw the ambassadors into deep pits.

Two years later, Darius sent an army to conquer Greece. His fleet crossed the Aegean Sea and landed at Marathon Bay, to the north of Athens. It was claimed that the Persians had six hundred ships and one hundred thousand men. The Athenian army was only about nine thousand strong.

According to the Greek historian Herodotus, the Athenian general Miltiades told an Olympic athlete called Pheidippides to run to Sparta to ask for help. Pheidippides ran the 250 miles (400 kilometres) to Sparta and back in four days. It was a wasted journey. The Spartans refused to come until the full moon, in five days' time.

Miltiades placed the strongest soldiers on the wings (on the right and left of his army), then the Athenians charged the huge Persian army. Although the centre of the Athenian army gave way, the two wings broke through the Persian lines and turned back to surround the enemy, who panicked and fled. Only 192 Greeks died, but 6,400 Persians were killed.

There is a legend that Pheidippides was told to run the 26 miles (42 kilometres) from Marathon to Athens with the good news. He ran all the way, gave the message and then died. Although probably untrue, this legend gave the modern 'marathon' race its name.

Above: Pheidippides (on the left) running to Sparta.

Far left: a Persian soldier and his equipment.

Below: the usual Greek dressing was to wind the two ends of the bandage round the wound in different directions and then to tie the ends. This soldier is having problems tying the knot because he has wound both ends of the bandage round the same way.

Thermopylae and Salamis

In 480 BC, Darius's son, Xerxes, invaded Greece with an army, one writer claimed, of five million men. Such a figure is impossible but, even so, Xerxes was so confident that when some Greek spies were captured he showed them his army and set them free.

Alarmed by the strength and size of the Persian army, 31 Greek city-states formed an alliance. A force of seven thousand soldiers, commanded by the Spartan king, Leonidas, confronted the Persian army at Thermopylae, a narrow strip of land between the mountains and the sea. However, a traitor showed the Persians a secret pass through the hills. Most of the Greeks retreated, but Leonidas and three hundred of his men stayed to face the Persians. They wrestled and combed their hair as Spartans always did before a battle. Then they fought to the death.

Next, the Persian army marched on Athens. The Athenians had sent all the women and children south, so the city was almost deserted. The Persians defeated the few defenders and burned Athens to the ground.

The Athenians, however, had realized that the best defence was to build a navy. Their fleet, with warships from other city-states, lay to the west of the city in the Straits of Salamis. Although the Persian navy trapped the Greek ships in the straits, in the battle that followed the Persian fleet was destroyed. Xerxes returned to Persia; Greece had survived.

A Greek warship rams a Persian ship at the battle of Salamis in 480 BC. The Greek fleet is made up of 310 triremes (see page 28). Each is commanded by a man under the age of 50 and has a crew of ten marines aged 20-30, four archers and 170 rowers.

Half the Greek navy lures the Persian fleet into battle in the narrow straits where it is difficult to move freely in the strong breeze. The other half then surprises them by attacking from the rear. The Persian ships are smaller and more manoeuvrable but the heavier Greek ships are able to ram and sink them.

Silver and Grain

Why did Xerxes, ruler of an empire that stretched 3,000 miles (5,000 kilometres) from Asia Minor to India, fail to conquer the small city-state of Athens? Greek historians claimed that the cause was the foolish pride of Xerxes, and the bravery of the Greek warriors.

Xerxes, however, was fighting far from home. His capital city of Susa was a three-months' journey away; it is remarkable that the Persians could mount an invasion at all.

Athens, at this time, was not a poor farming community but a powerful city-state. In 483 BC a rich vein of silver had been discovered in southern Attica, which paid for the Athenian fleet. In addition, Athens could call on the other city-states for support.

Athens was also a centre for trade. Most Athenian merchants were *metoikoi* (see page 7). The poet Hermippos listed the goods they brought in: 'Hellespont mackerel and fish of all kinds; Thessaly puddings and ribs of beef…From Egypt, rigging, sails and papyrus…African ivory in plenty at a price; from Rhodes, raisins…from Carthage, carpets…'. The most important trade was in grain, for Attica could never have fed the population of Athens. In 335 BC, a Greek writer claimed that the Crimea alone sent 17,000 tons of wheat a year to Athens.

Left: a scribe lists Athens' imports. Opposite page: leather from Sicily; a silver coffee pot from Asia Minor; tin from Britain; dyes from Syria; grain from Sicily, Cyrene, Egypt and the Black Sea; French wine; Hellespont mackerel; copper from Cyprus; ivory and cloth from Africa; and, above, wood from Macedonia. To pay for these, Athens exports (above, top) jewellery, pottery, olives and grapes.

Athenian Democracy

What is democracy? More than two thousand years after the time of the ancient Greeks, the American president Abraham Lincoln defined it as 'government of the people, by the people, for the people'. Today, many countries claim to be democracies.

The idea of democracy was invented in Athens in about 500 BC. Athenian democracy, however, was not like modern democracy. In Athens, only citizens had the right to vote and only adult males could be citizens. Women, slaves and the *metoikoi* (see page 7) could not be citizens and had no say in the government.

Neither did the Athenians have elected members of parliament, as we do today. Athens was a direct democracy; the citizens themselves decided such matters as whether to go to war, or put unsuccessful generals to death. They met on a hill in Athens called the Pnyx and voted by a show of hands.

The people's assembly, the *ekklesia*, met 40 times a year. It was supposed to meet early in the day, and every male citizen was supposed to attend; our word idiot comes from the Greek word meaning someone who cares only about his personal affairs, not those of the state. In practice, however, perhaps only six thousand (one-tenth) of the citizens attended regularly and one writer complained that when he arrived on time he was the only one there! It was often noon before everyone had assembled.

The meeting started with the sacrifice of a black pig, followed by prayers. Rain was seen as a bad omen and the meeting would be cancelled. Everybody had the right to speak, and the crowd interrupted and yelled abuse whenever they disagreed. If you supported the speaker, you called him a *rhetor* (orator, see above right); if you opposed him, you referred to him as a *demagogue* (mob leader). The historian Thucydides described such a

Pericles, an Athenian leader of the fifth century BC (below), was not their ruler. His power came only from his ability to influence the *ekklesia*. 'Persuasion lived on his lips,' wrote one Greek poet. 'He cast a spell on us.'

The meetings of the *ekklesia* were organized by a council of five hundred and a sub-committee whose chairman was chosen by lot and served for one day only. The remarkable result was that, at some time in his life, one in three Athenian citizens found himself, for one proud day, in charge of the city-state.

Greeks from other city-states claimed that democracy gave power to poor men who

man striding about the platform, shouting, waving his arms and slapping his thigh.

The Athenians never let a citizen become so powerful that he could take complete control of the city-state. Generals were elected. Other officials were chosen by lot, so their appointment was pure chance. After a year they had to present their accounts in public, whereupon anybody could take them to court on a charge of misconduct. People scratched the names of any citizens they thought had become too powerful on small pieces of pottery called *ostraka* (below). On a particular day, these were cast into a box in the market-place. If a total of six thousand *ostraka* were cast, the person with most votes against him would be ostracized (forced to leave the city).

were unfit to rule. They thought that Athens was full of dangerous ideas.

Athenians, however, were proud of their democracy. Freedom of speech encouraged playwrights (see page 33) and philosophers (see pages 34-35). Pericles said that democracy allowed the cleverest people, even if they were poor, to become state officials. Rich and poor alike, having a stake in the state, were happy to work and live and die for it.

This helps to explain why the Athenians defeated the Persians and why, in the time of Pericles, Athens gained an empire.

Slaves who act as the Athenian police force go through the town marking latecomers to the *ekklesia* with ropes dipped in red dye. Any man who arrives with a red mark on his cloak is fined.

The Athenian Empire

The Greek victory at Salamis did not end the wars with Persia. Xerxes left an army in Greece, which was defeated in 479 BC.

The next year, on the island of Delos, Athens and a number of other city-states formed an alliance called the Delian League. The aim of the League was to raid Persian lands, to replace the money spent on the recent war. For the next 30 years the League's forces attacked the Persian Empire.

At about the same time, the Athenians repaired the damage done by the Persians.

First they rebuilt the walls around Athens and its harbour town, Piraeus, about 5 miles (8 kilometres) away. Then they built walls (the 'Long Walls') to protect the vital strip of land linking Piraeus and Athens. The work took 20 years, but when it was finished Athens was a strongly fortified city.

Slowly, the Delian League began to turn into the Athenian Empire (see map). Each year the Athenians collected a tribute of ships or money from the member-states. In 454 BC, they moved the League's treasury from Delos to Athens.

The other states in the League were forced to worship Athene. Pressure was put on them to become democracies (see page 26) and they were told to hold important court cases in Athens. When the island of Thasos tried to leave the League in 465 BC, the Athenians destroyed the city's walls, confiscated its navy and made it pay a large sum of money.

The period 463-429 BC, when Pericles was the Athenians' leader, came to be known as the Golden Age of Athens.

Right: the basis of Athenian power is a navy of triremes (boats with three banks of oars). If any state fails to pay the tribute, Athens sends a trireme with two officials who demand payment.

Left: an official counts the tribute money, checking it against the amount written down on the wax tablet.

Art and Architecture

Athens was the centre of an empire, so it should be a city 'worthy of admiration', said Pericles. After 450 BC, therefore, many fine buildings were constructed. Most were temples dedicated to the gods, but the Athenians also built a large *oideion* (concert

hall) and a number of impressive *stoas* (covered walkways). Pericles borrowed money from the temple treasuries, which he repaid out of the tribute taken from the empire's member-states.

The Athenians were lovers of beauty. The philosopher Plato thought that the law should only allow the construction of graceful buildings 'so that our young men may

drink in good from every side'. Public buildings were constructed of local white marble from Mount Pentelikon, a few miles to the north-east of Athens. From Mount Hymettus, east of Athens, came a reddish rock that was a natural concrete, which the builders used for the foundations. The finished buildings were decorated with friezes and statues, and then they were brightly painted in gold, blue, green and red.

Between 447 and 432 BC, the Athenians built a temple dedicated to the goddess Athene (see page 13). It was called the Parthenon and its architect was Ictinus.

Greek architects thought that the arch was unsuitable for large buildings, so Ictinus used flat beams, supported on columns. However, he used several optical illusions so that the huge building would not appear misproportioned to the observer on the ground. If the long sides of the building had been straight they would have looked as if they were sagging, so Ictinus made them curve up slightly in the middle – the centres are 11 centimetres (4.4 inches) higher than the ends. In the same way, each column becomes thinner towards the top so that it seems straight to someone looking up at it. The columns also lean slightly inwards so that the building does not seem top-heavy; if they were extended upwards by 1.5 miles (2.4 kilometres), they would eventually meet!

Below: the Acropolis (meaning upper city) is the rocky hill overlooking Athens. The largest temple is the Parthenon. The temple on the left is the Erekhtheion where, every four years during the festival of *Panathenaea* (see page 14), the Athenians bring a new robe for Athene's statue.

The rest of the Acropolis is covered with temples, altars, statues, memorial stones and storehouses. Here also is the State Treasury of Athens. On a pedestal in front of the wall in the centre of the Acropolis stands a huge bronze statue of Athene. Athenian sailors know they are almost home when they see on the horizon the glint of the sun on her helmet and spear.

Over the centuries Greek sculpture develops greatly. Early Greek figures are known as *kouroi* (*c.* 600 BC). They are inspired by Egyptian sculptures and show their subjects standing stiffly, one foot in front of the other (far left). A century later (*c.* 490 BC) the fallen warrior on a Greek temple looks more life-like, although the position is still not wholly natural (below left).

By the first century BC Greek sculptors are able to use their understanding of the muscles beneath the skin to achieve a feeling of reality. We know the name of the sculptor of the resting boxer (right) because he has signed his name on the glove. He is an Athenian: Apollonios, son of Nestor.

The Theatre

The Athenians invented drama. It developed from ancient festivals in honour of the god Dionysus. Competitions were held at two religious festivals, in January and March, when plays were performed and judged.

The first plays consisted of only a single speaker, with a chorus of about 12-15 men, who danced and sang to fill out the details of the story. The Athenian writer Aeschylus (c. 525-456 BC) had the idea of using a second actor. Later writers wrote plays with more characters but they were only allowed a maximum of three actors, so each actor had to play a number of parts. They wore a different mask for each character. Although plays were performed only twice a year in Athens, there were professional actors who toured Greece during the rest of the year.

Early Greek plays told the stories of the gods and heroes (the tragedies). Later plays were about everyday life (the comedies). In

Athens, where there was freedom of speech, the writers of comedies mocked not only the leaders of the time but the gods and, even more dangerously, the audience. The comic writer Aristophanes (*c.* 450-388 BC) often also included a few lines attacking other playwrights (writers of plays). In *Knights* (425 BC), he portrayed his rival Kratinos as a drunken failure, and won first prize at the festival. The next year Kratinos wrote a play called *Flask*, also portraying himself as a drunken failure. He had the last laugh. He won first prize; Aristophanes came last!

The plays were very popular; the theatre of Dionysus in Athens seated fourteen thousand people. Nevertheless, audiences threw food and even stones if they disliked a play. One actor had so many figs thrown at him that it was said he could have started a fruit stall.

In the *Oresteia* tragedies by Aeschylus the hero Agamemnon is trapped in a net by his wife and killed because he has sacrificed their child to the gods. The actors wear large masks and thick-soled shoes so that the audience can see them more clearly.

Knowledge and Philosophy

As Greek colonists travelled to different areas of the Mediterranean, they met people with completely different beliefs and ideas. Historians think that this led them to investigate and study. Certainly, the Greeks loved to find out new things. The philosopher Socrates was told by the Oracle at Delphi that he was the wisest man in Greece. This puzzled him; *he* thought he knew very little. In the end he decided that his wisdom lay in the fact that he *knew* that he knew very little, and was trying to learn more. 'A life without asking questions is no life at all,' he said.

The Greeks were the first people to write books on geography and history (see page 62). Pythagoras, who lived from *c.* 580-500 BC, studied mathematics and geometry; his theory about the sides of a right-angled triangle is still taught in schools. A Greek scientist, Archimedes (*c.* 287-212 BC), realized as he climbed into his bath (below) why things float in water. His famous cry, *'Eureka!'* ('I have found it!'), is still remembered.

Anaximander (*c.* 610-546 BC) said that the Earth was not flat as many people thought, but a solid body hanging in space. Greek philosophers realized that the world was millions of years old and that fossils were creatures from an earlier age. Other Greek writers suggested that all matter was composed of tiny atoms which were too small to be seen. All these ideas were lost during the Middle Ages, and it was more than two thousand years before western scientists realized that they were right.

Unlike anyone before them, the Greeks looked for rational (common sense) answers to their questions. Many doubted the stories of the gods. Did the gods look like human beings? Probably not, thought the Greek writer Xenophanes (*c.* 560-478 BC): 'The Ethiopians say that their gods are black… If horses could draw, they would draw their gods looking like horses.' Some doubted whether the gods existed at all: 'Zeus? What Zeus? There isn't any Zeus!' says a character in a play by Aristophanes.

The Greeks developed logic and many of the rules of argument. Argument from probability (asking, 'Is it likely?') is still used by lawyers in courts of law. Above all, the Greeks realized that there are two sides to every question: 'Sickness is bad for the sick, but good for the doctor; a worn-out shoe is bad for the owner but good for the cobbler.' This idea of opposites became very important in Greek thought.

The Greeks loved to struggle with complicated ideas. One argument 'proved' that your father was a dog: if a dog has puppies he is a *father*, and if he is *your* dog, he must be *your father*. A mathematician called Zeno (*c.* 495-430 BC) 'proved' that Achilles could never catch a tortoise if he gave it a 100-metre (110-yard) start – even if he ran a hundred times faster. The argument involved a clever trick using fractions. While Achilles ran 100 metres, said Zeno, the tortoise could travel one metre; then while Achilles ran that metre, the tortoise could travel one centimetre; and while Achilles ran that centimetre, the tortoise could travel 0.01 centimetre…and so on. The tortoise would always be a fraction ahead!

You may be able to spot the mistakes in these two conundrums (puzzles).

Many Greek philosophers went to live in Athens. Some became famous, for example the eccentric thinker Diogenes (c. 412-320 BC), who showed his hatred of worldly possessions by living in a barrel. Aristophanes mocked the fashion for asking questions such as 'Why?' and 'What?' Even ordinary men, he wrote, have barely arrived home before they start to scream, 'Why isn't my jug here? What's the matter? Who's eaten my olives?'

Most people, however, still believed in the gods, and regarded the philosophers as dangerous people. In 399 BC the Athenians found Socrates guilty of refusing to honour the gods and leading young people astray. He committed suicide by drinking hemlock (poison).

Socrates' pupil Plato (c. 427-347 BC) opens a school of philosophy in Athens. He uses Socrates' method of teaching, asking his pupils questions.

Doctors

After the sixth century BC, temple-hospitals were set up in many city-states. They were called *asklepeia* after Asklepios, the god of medicine. Patients believed that the god came to cure them during the night. Historians suspect that the patients were drugged, then treated while they slept.

After about 460 BC, however, Greek doctors adopted a complicated theory of healing, based on the idea that matter was made up of four elements: fire, earth, water and air (see the modern diagram, right). They believed that the body was composed of four humours (liquids): blood, phlegm, yellow bile (vomit)

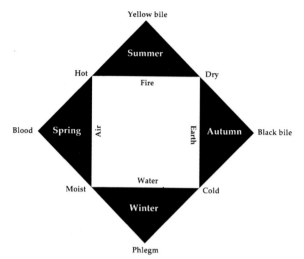

and black bile (excrement). Disease occurred if the humours became unbalanced. In winter, for instance, if a person became cold and wet,

his body would produce too much phlegm and he would catch a cold.

Using this theory of the four humours, Greek doctors developed a system of 'natural healing' by the use of opposites (see page 34). The cure for a cold, for instance, was to keep the patient hot and dry, beside the fire. The Greeks expanded these ideas into a full programme for health. In the hot, dry summer, people were told to balance the humours by taking long, cool drinks. In winter they were recommended to keep warm by taking brisk walks. Many *asklepeia* became health resorts, with gymnasia, swimming baths and running tracks.

The Greek doctor Hippocrates, sometimes called the Father of Medicine, invented a system of examination called clinical observation, which is still used by doctors today. He demanded that doctors should be well-trained, calm and caring, 'pure and holy in life and practice'. In many countries, doctors still take the Hippocratic oath, promising to treat the sick to the best of their ability.

This boy has pains in his arm and side. The doctor examines him and decides that the problem is an excess of blood. He bleeds the patient using a bleeding cup. The cup is heated and placed over a scratch on the boy's arm. As the cup cools, a vacuum is created and blood is sucked out into it.

To the right, an assistant is about to treat another patient for backache by standing on him. A slave brings a flask of urine for the doctor to examine. Around the room are plants and herbs which the doctor prescribes.

37

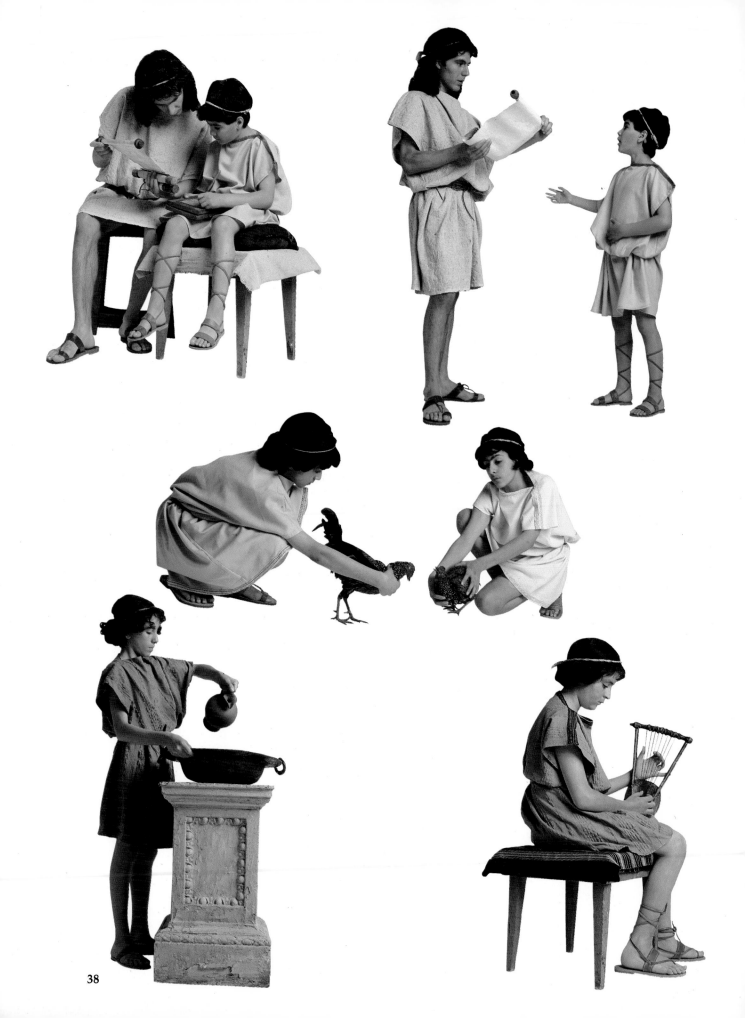

The Boy Becomes a Citizen

Greek women gave birth at home. In Athens, three female neighbours and a midwife would be present. The midwife knew the rituals needed to obtain the help of the birth goddesses, but could do little if problems arose with the birth. If progress was slow, the midwife wrapped the girl in a blanket and shook her up and down. Perhaps one in five women died in childbirth. 'I would rather fight three times in battle than give birth once,' says Medea, a woman in a Greek play.

When a child was born, the helpers gave a traditional *ololuge* (birth-cry). Most parents wanted sons; baby boys seem to have been kept and loved, even if they were weak or disabled. Midwives arranged adoptions, taking any unwanted infants to mothers whose babies had died.

Most Greeks would have agreed with the wet-nurse in one play, who remarks that 'children are brainless things'. The Greek word *nepios* (infant) also meant careless and ignorant. Education was therefore considered to be very important for boys. In Athens they went to school at about the age of seven, and even poor pupils stayed until they were fourteen. Rich children went on to study astronomy, geometry, geography, history and rhetoric (public speaking). Strict laws governed schools and the teachers' behaviour. Occasionally, a pupil who thought he was not being properly taught would beat his teacher.

At the age of 18 an Athenian boy began two years' military training. He wore a broad-brimmed hat and a black travelling cloak (below). When he had completed his training, he offered a sacrifice and was put on the register of the *ekklesia* as a citizen.

Top left to bottom right: an Athenian pupil learns mathematics, reading and writing; a slave makes sure that he does not giggle or sit cross-legged. He sings the poems of Homer to learn them by heart. He has time off for games such as cock-fighting but, in more serious moments, he prepares for the family sacrifice and plays the lyre. His older brother learns to speak like a *rhetor*. All pupils do athletics training.

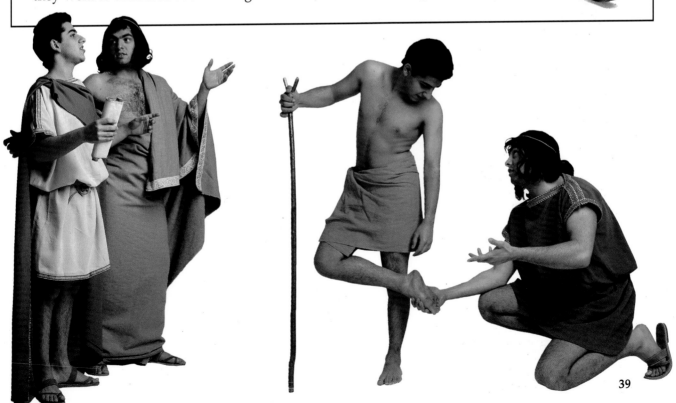

39

The Girl Becomes a Mother

Girl babies were often abandoned. 'If you bear a child,' a Greek soldier wrote to his wife, 'keep it if it is a boy. If it is a girl, cast it out.' In about 220 BC, a census (count) of the inhabitants of Miletus, a Greek city in Asia Minor, recorded 169 boys and only 46 girls.

At about the age of nine, a few Athenian girls were sent to 'act the bear' for a month in the Temple of Artemis, the goddess of hunting. They performed strange religious rituals which involved running around wildly. Some teenage girls joined the choirs which sang at religious festivals. In general, however, girls were 'given as little food as possible [and] were expected to keep their mouths shut and to attend to their wool'. In a Greek novel written to show husbands how to control their wives, the 15-year-old wife 'had lived under the strictest discipline, and had been taught to see, hear or ask as little as possible'. She did, however, know how to weave cloth and was a well-trained cook.

Fifteen was a common age for an Athenian girl to marry. Her husband would be nearer 30. The girl's father arranged her marriage, and paid the bridegroom a dowry. Most marriages took place in the winter month of Gamelion, the 'month of marriages'. The girl gave her toys to the Temple of Artemis, cut her hair, took a ritual bath in holy water and ate a last meal with her family. Then, at night, her husband and his friends arrived and took her away in a chariot (above). There was no wedding ceremony, although the groom's friends sang songs called hymns (after Hymen, the god of marriage).

Most Greek brides were terrified. One woman wrote: 'We are thrown out and sold away from our household gods and our parents. We go to the homes of men who may be strangers, foreigners, joyless or brutal. And once we are yoked to our husbands, we are forced to praise them and say all is well.'

A wife's tasks: training her child to use the pot (opposite page, top left) and bottle-feeding the baby (centre left). Bottom, left to right: she must tidy the house and make offerings to Zeus and Apollo on an altar in the courtyard. One of the few chances she has to meet other women is when she goes to fetch water.

Sending a girl to school is like 'giving extra poison to a dangerous snake', says one Greek writer. Instead, Greek girls stay at home and learn the skills they will need when they marry. Below, left to right: a young girl is taught to grind corn. An older girl is shown by her mother how to spin and weave.

At Home

Men had complete control over women in ancient Greece. The hero of one of Homer's poems gives orders to his mother: 'Go back into the house and attend to your weaving and spinning. I will do the talking. For I am the ruler in this household,' he says.

Poor women had to work. Wealthy Greek wives, however, spent most of their lives in the *gunaikeion*, the women's room. A woman was supposed to rush to the *gunaikeion* if she met a man who was not a member of her family, even if she was in the courtyard of her own house.

'A wife's business is to stay indoors and supervise the servants, do the household accounts, make the clothes and see that the grain is dry,' was the advice given in one book. It was shameful for a woman to be seen in public, except at a funeral or religious festival. Wealthy men hired chaperones to accompany their wives if they had to go out.

Women and slaves did the routine jobs of society. This allowed the men to go to war, take part in politics and visit the agora (see page 49). Few Athenian men, however, thought women were important: 'One man's life is worth thousands of women,' says a Greek heroine, in a play written by a man.

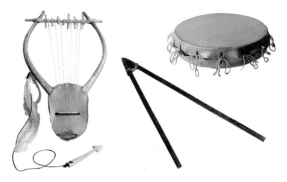

In the men's apartment in the house, the husband and his friends enjoy a simple but good meal. The first course consists of sea urchins with olives, garlic and radishes. For the main course there is tuna cooked in salt water, with a stuffing of herbs. Greeks like to mix sweet and sour tastes, and the third course is meat, flavoured with cheese and aniseed. Vegetables, garlic, fruit and dandelion salad are also served. At the end of the meal, the guests eat the pastries for which Athens is famous.

The men drink heavily and become drunk. It is a Greek joke that the first toast is to Dionysus, the god of wine, the second to love and the third to arguments and fighting. Girls are invited, but not wives. Athenian men prefer to chat to educated foreign women. Known as *hetairai* (companions), they entertain the men by dancing and playing musical instruments such as the lyre, *aulos* (pipe) and tambourine (above). Later, the women are sent away and the men discuss philosophy.

Craftsmen and Traders

Some craftsmen became very rich, especially those in trades which supplied the warring armies of Greece. The architects, painters and sculptors who worked on the Parthenon (see page 30) were also highly paid. At the other end of the scale were the tradesmen who sold 'coal, figs, leather, spoons, books, buns and seed', and the poor people who waited at the Market Mound in Athens to be hired as labourers.

Greek philosophers, however, despised everybody who worked for a living. They taught that a citizen should devote himself to war, politics, athletics, hunting and philosophy. Tradesmen, they said, were uneducated and had no time for politics; craftsmen (who worked indoors) were flabby and unhealthy; shopkeepers (who sold at a profit) were no better than thieves. Aristophanes mocked the blacksmiths, cobblers and armourers who had to leap out of bed as soon as the cock crowed.

This attitude led many Greeks to try to live on the income from their farms. In Athens, trade and crafts were left to the *metoikoi* (see page 7).

It is ironic that, without the craftsmen, the wealthy would not have been able to live as they did. 'Every skill and invention of mankind is at your service,' a character called Rich is told in a play by Aristophanes. 'For you one of us sits making shoes. Others work in bronze, wood and gold. Another washes cloth. Another washes skins.'

Below: this pot has been thrown (shaped) on a potter's wheel and lightly baked in a kiln. Now the painter decorates and glazes it, ready for refiring in the kiln.

Above, left to right: Greek skill in pottery develops through the centuries. Early designs (*c.* 750 BC) consist of patterns and silhouettes. By the sixth century BC the vase painters are designing vivid scenes from the Greek myths, drawing black figures on a red clay-coloured background. Half a century later they use black for the background. They draw details of clothing and muscles on the red clay-coloured figures portraying scenes of everyday life in Greece.

Slaves

Most slaves were barbarians, captured in war or by pirates. Occasionally, babies that had been abandoned were rescued and sold by slave traders. All the children of slaves were born into slavery.

Prices varied from 72 drachmas for an infant, to more than 300 drachmas for an educated Syrian male (a drachma was the daily wage of a skilled worker). One rich Athenian owned a thousand slaves, whom he hired out at one obol (one-sixth of a drachma) per day. It has been estimated that slaves formed one-third of the population of Athens in the fifth century BC.

House slaves did most of the menial tasks and helped the women to look after the children and old people. Many slaves laboured alongside the foreigners and poor Athenians on the buildings of the Acropolis. Others worked in the craftsmen's workshops. One sword-maker, for instance, employed 32 slaves, and the orator Lysias (see page 16) owned a shield factory which had a work-force of 120 slaves. The city of Athens employed three hundred slaves as its police force. There were perhaps forty thousand slaves in the state silver mines, where they worked in terrible conditions.

Not all slaves were badly treated or worked in lowly jobs. Some held important positions as clerks, bankers and ships' captains. If they saved carefully, they could buy their freedom. In the fourth century BC, a slave named Pasion married his master's widow, took over his master's banking business and became a citizen of Athens.

Greek philosophers argued about whether slavery was natural or unnatural. The comic writer Crates, however, joked that slavery would only come to an end when the cup washed itself out, the food cooked itself, and the hot water came straight from the pipes.

Division of labour in a shoe workshop: one slave cuts the leather round the foot of a young customer, another stitches the leather and a third rounds off the shoes. The slave on the left is waiting to take the boy home.

48

In the Agora

In the morning most male citizens who did not have to work would go to the agora, an open space in the centre of Athens. Around the agora were the army headquarters, the records office, a prison and a public notice-board for new laws, forthcoming legal cases and lists of those needed for service in the army. Nearby was the Royal Stoa, where many of the laws of Athens were carved in stone, and the Painted Stoa, which was covered with murals showing the history of the city.

The lawcourts were also in the agora. An Athenian court case was noisy and chaotic. It started with prayers, then the charge was read. There were no lawyers; defendants (accused people) spoke for themselves. They were timed with a water clock (see page 63) and had to stop when the water ran out. Witnesses, usually friends or relatives, were not cross-examined. Although there was a magistrate who tried to keep order, there was no judge; the jurors acted as both judge and jury. Jurors were paid, so there was always a great crowd of volunteers; up to 2,500 turned up every day. They interrupted and shouted down unpopular defendants. When everyone had spoken, the jurors voted by dropping pebbles (called voting ballots) into a pot. If the verdict was guilty, the jury voted again, this time on the sentence. The verdict was given on the same day as the trial, so justice was quick, even if it was often unfair.

The agora is always full of people gossiping, gathering for an ostracism (see page 27) or hoping to be chosen for jury service. Farmers and craftsmen have set up their stalls beneath the trees; the Greek word *agoradzo* means to buy. Here also are the characters mocked by the writer Theophrastus: the over-confident man asking his army officer what his orders will be the day after tomorrow, and the chatterbox delaying the children by showing them how to wrestle. Everybody knows Cleonymus, the fat man, and Cleisthenes in his fancy clothes. Playwrights can get a laugh just by mentioning their names.

Old Age and Death

There were relatively few old people in Greece. Although some philosophers are reported to have lived to the age of 100, studies of skeletons show that most men died when they were about 44 years old. Women, worn out by childbirth, often died even younger, at about 35.

In Athens, if a man lived long enough, it was customary for him to retire at 60 when his son got married. He handed over control of the farm to his son. By law the son had to give his aged parents food, a room and a decent burial. Women were classed as old when they could no longer have children and were therefore considered less necessary to society. One of the benefits of this was that they were at last allowed to go out alone in public.

The city paid a pension to the parents of men who had died in battle, and to widows who had given birth to male children. Many aged poor people, however, had to look after themselves. Old men could earn a little money doing jury service and old women acted as professional mourners at funerals or as midwives and wet-nurses. When slaves became old and sick, they were sometimes thrown out and left to die.

Greeks hated old age, with its sicknesses

and senility. Old people were thought to be 'ugly outside and dirty-minded within… hateful to young men and despicable to women'. In the Greek myths, Geras, the god of old age, was the son of Night and the brother of Doom and Death.

Nevertheless, the playwright Euripides said, 'it is silly the way old men complain about old age and long life; if death comes close, not one of them wants to die'.

The funeral is held on the third day after death. The corpse has been washed, anointed, wrapped in a shroud and garlanded. It is laid on a bier and carried in procession to a cemetery outside the walls of the city. Sometimes the body is burned on a pyre. Here, however, it will be buried in a grave which will be marked with a *stele* (a gravestone, shown above left).

Each year the family will go to the tomb and sprinkle oil on it from a *lekythos* (above right).

Plague and War

In 459-445 BC and (after a short peace) in 431-404, there was war between Athens and her allies (supporters), and the Spartans and their allies. For years there was stalemate. Sparta could not defeat the Athenian navy; Athens could not defeat Sparta's army.

In 430-429 BC, however, Athens suffered a terrible plague. Many leading men were victims of the disease; Pericles died of it in 429 BC. Noblemen complained that trades-men and merchants, some with no land at all, were coming into the government. The Athenians lost confidence in their gods. 'Prayers and oracles were useless…men belittled all sacred and holy things,' wrote the historian Thucydides, who witnessed these events. Society collapsed. 'Corpses lay where they died on top of each other, and the dying lurched around the streets crying for water…Burial rites were ignored; people threw corpses on to other people's pyres.'

In 413 and 405 BC the Athenians suffered two disastrous naval defeats. The Spartans entered the city, demolished the Long Walls (see page 28) and took over the Athenian Empire.

The states of Greece were just as hostile to a Spartan empire, however, as they had been towards Athens. In 371 and 362 BC the 'invincible' Spartan army was twice defeated by the Thebans.

It seemed that no city-state could conquer all of Greece. As soon as one state grew stronger, the others united to destroy it; the Greek states had fought themselves to a stand-still. Because of this, they were conquered by a new power from the north – Philip II, ruler of the kingdom of Macedon.

In 338 BC Philip invaded Greece, decisively defeating an army of Thebans and Athenians which tried to stop him.

Each unit of Greek soldiers fights in a tightly packed group called a phalanx. The stone frieze (below) shows two forces of Greek soldiers at war. In the town, a woman cries out in grief.

The Greeks, however, are no match for the Macedonians. Each Macedonian soldier (right) wears a leather jerkin. His helmet, shield and greaves (leg armour) are made of bronze. He carries a sword and a *sarissa* (pike), which is 5.5 metres (18 feet) long. To the right are a number of leather pouches in which he carries his rations, equipment and stones for his sling.

Philip and Alexander

Macedon was a kingdom to the north of Greece. The Macedonians were shepherds with primitive customs; they spoke Greek with such a strong accent that the Greeks could not understand them.

In 359 BC, Philip II had become king of Macedon. As king, he had total power over his people; the Macedonians believed that he was a descendant of Zeus. Philip built new towns and 'moved peoples into them as he decided'. On one occasion, he sent to his new towns twenty thousand Scythian women and children, who were prisoners of war. 'My father took you over as nomads and shepherds; he gave you cloaks to wear instead of sheepskins, he made you the inhabitants of cities, and gave you good laws and customs,' Philip's son Alexander was later to tell his troops.

Philip admired Greek civilization. He hired the Greek philosopher Aristotle as tutor for his son. Alexander was a fierce boy, envious of his father's success.

Philip developed a strong army. He trained his men by sending them on 37-mile (60-kilometre) marches with heavy back packs. Unlike the Greeks, the Macedonians made use of cavalry (soldiers on horseback) in their warfare. In 338 BC, Alexander became

the commander of Philip's cavalry.

By 337 BC Philip had gained a small empire in the Balkans. That year he forced the Greek city-states to join a Greek League, with himself as *hegemon* (leader). Philip did not rob or enslave the people he conquered. He just required the captured country to help him in his wars. Thus his empire grew. Philip's reign marks the beginning of the shift of power away from the Middle East – the 'cradle of civilization' – to Europe.

In 336 BC, Philip and the Greek League declared war on Persia. Just when his army was ready, however, Philip was murdered by an officer of his court.

After Philip's death, Alexander was proclaimed king by the Macedonian soldiers, who marched between the two halves of a sacrificed dog to show their loyalty. He became *hegemon* of the Greek League. When the Thebans revolted, Alexander destroyed the city and sold its inhabitants into slavery. Then he went to war against the Persian Empire, defeating the Persian king, Darius III, at the battles of Issus (333 BC) and Gaugamela (331 BC). A year later Darius was murdered by his own bodyguards. Alexander sat on Darius's throne and commented: 'So this is what it is like to be an emperor.'

A Roman mosaic, *c.* AD 79, shows Alexander (far left) and Darius (in his chariot, centre) at the battle of Issus.

Alexander the Great

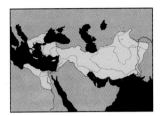

For eleven years Alexander and his troops marched all over the Middle East. He conquered every province he passed through and set up new cities, at least 16 of which he called Alexandria. During one of his sieges, he also found a wife when he captured a beautiful young princess called Roxana. By the time of his death in 323 BC, at the age of 32, he was the ruler of a vast empire (see map).

Alexander's troops came from every part of his empire, but they loved and admired him. When he was dying of a fever, they queued up to file past him. Feebly, Alexander raised his head to each one.

Even during Alexander's lifetime myths were growing up about him. It was thought that so great a man must be a god. One story claimed that Alexander had asked an oracle in Egypt, 'Am I the Son of God?' and had been told, 'You are.'

Other stories were less complimentary. It was claimed that he was a drunkard, who needed two days' sleep to recover from his drinking bouts; that he kept Darius's harem of 365 women, 'one for every day of the year'; that he killed a friend who refused to worship him as a god; and that on one occasion he massacred eighty thousand Indians.

Alexander's deeds prove that he was a brave and brilliant general, who could win victories with very few losses. He was also a genius at organization who, for 11 years and thousands of miles from home, supplied one hundred thousand men with provisions and all the materials of war. Paying them was not such a problem; we are told that it took five thousand camels and twenty thousand mules to carry the loot from one Persian city alone!

Below: In 326 BC, Alexander reaches India, where he defeats a huge Indian army, which includes 200 war-elephants. This coin shows him on horseback, attacking an elephant with his *sarissa*. Maddened with the pain of the Macedonian arrows and pikes, the elephants turn and trample their own men. Alexander was the first Greek to have his image on a coin – an honour previously reserved only for the gods. Main picture: Alexander wants to go further into India, but his troops refuse to follow him. He sulks in his tent for three days, but in the end is forced to turn back.

Alexandria

When Alexander died, his generals divided his empire between them. Where Alexander's armies had conquered, Greek traders followed, setting up small colonies from Egypt to India. Greek became the most common language of the Middle East. Greek ways were copied by the people of the conquered countries. This influence is called Hellenism by historians.

During Alexander's campaigns in Persia, a young architect called Dinocrates had followed the army, hoping to be given some work. Having no success, he dressed up in a lion's skin and carried a club. He was noticed straight away! He was brought to Alexander, who asked him to plan the new city of Alexandria in Egypt.

The city, which had half a million inhabitants, became the centre of Hellenism. It was laid out on a grid pattern, including an agora and a large park planted with plane trees. It had a double harbour, with a lighthouse on the offshore island of Pharos (this idea was copied all over the world; the French word for lighthouse is still *phare*). Alexandria was especially famous for its silverware and papyrus (reeds used to make a type of paper).

In the third century BC the Egyptian ruler Ptolemy I Soter founded a library at Alexandria. The post of librarian was held by some of the world's most brilliant scholars. Alexandria became a literary centre; we know the names of 1,100 Hellenistic writers. They copied and edited all the classic Greek poems and plays. In addition, they translated famous books written in other languages, such as the Jewish Old Testament. When Callimachus of Cyrene was librarian, he had all the items in the library catalogued, including about seven hundred thousand scrolls.

Ptolemy I Soter also built a museum in Alexandria. This was not a place to keep ancient things, but a research centre where the Muses (daughters of Zeus, who inspired scholars) were honoured. Many scientists went to Alexandria to further their studies.

The Greek astronomer Hipparchus (who died *c.* 127 BC) calculated the length of the solar year. Modern scientists, using the most sophisticated instruments, have discovered that he was wrong, but by only 6 minutes and 14 seconds.

A scientist called Eratosthenes (*c.* 276-194 BC) heard that in Syene, in southern Egypt, once a year at midday the sun's rays shone straight down into the village well. This showed that the sun was directly overhead.

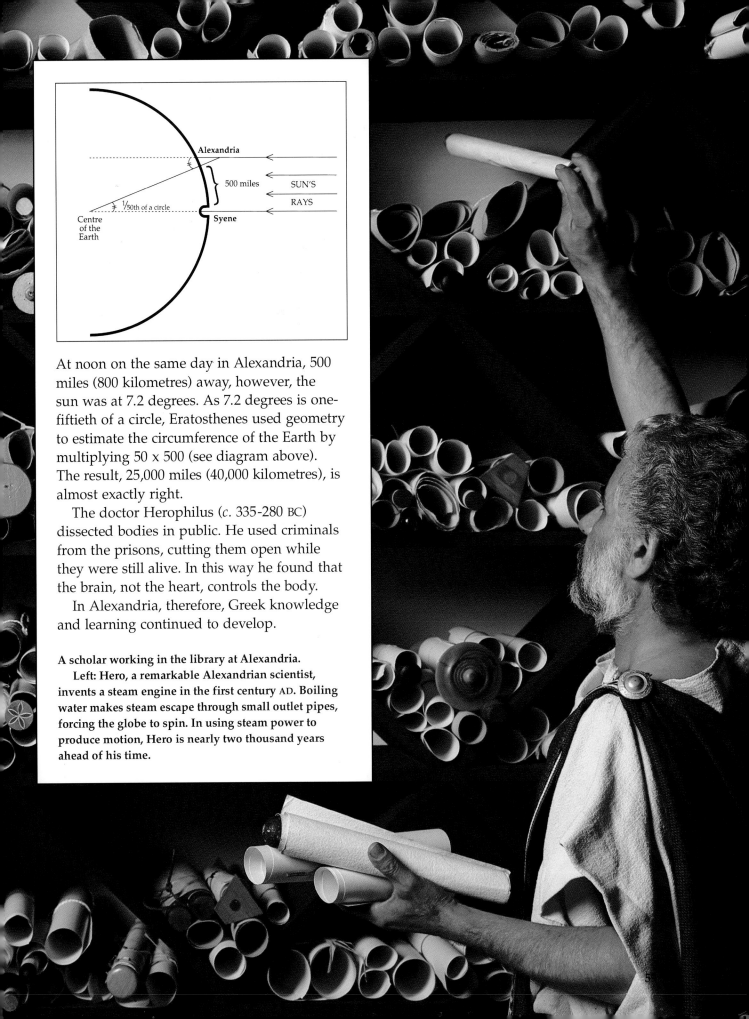

At noon on the same day in Alexandria, 500 miles (800 kilometres) away, however, the sun was at 7.2 degrees. As 7.2 degrees is one-fiftieth of a circle, Eratosthenes used geometry to estimate the circumference of the Earth by multiplying 50 x 500 (see diagram above). The result, 25,000 miles (40,000 kilometres), is almost exactly right.

The doctor Herophilus (*c.* 335-280 BC) dissected bodies in public. He used criminals from the prisons, cutting them open while they were still alive. In this way he found that the brain, not the heart, controls the body.

In Alexandria, therefore, Greek knowledge and learning continued to develop.

A scholar working in the library at Alexandria.
Left: Hero, a remarkable Alexandrian scientist, invents a steam engine in the first century AD. Boiling water makes steam escape through small outlet pipes, forcing the globe to spin. In using steam power to produce motion, Hero is nearly two thousand years ahead of his time.

The diagram labels: Alexandria, 500 miles, SUN'S RAYS, 1/50th of a circle, Syene, Centre of the Earth

Rome

At the time of Alexander's successes in the Middle East, Rome was a small but aggressive state in central Italy.

During the next two centuries, however, the Romans became more powerful. First they conquered the Greek colonies in southern Italy and Sicily. Then, in 168 BC, they defeated the Macedonians. They captured one thousand slaves, including a young historian called Polybius. After accompanying a Roman general on his campaigns, Polybius became convinced that the well-disciplined Roman army could not be beaten.

At first, the Greeks welcomed the defeat of the Macedonians. In 146 BC, however, the Romans invaded Greece and destroyed the wealthy city of Corinth, carrying off many priceless works of art. Greece became a Roman province.

It would seem from their writings that the Romans despised the Greeks. They believed that the Greek Empire had collapsed because the Greeks had become soft and used to luxury. Nevertheless, the Romans copied the Greek way of life. They adopted Greek architecture, Greek literature and Greek theatre. The Emperor Nero attended the Olympic Games, although most Romans preferred their own, more bloodthirsty games. Greek slaves taught the children of wealthy Romans, and were employed by powerful men as secretaries and accountants. Greek doctors were as popular as the athletics champions of the time. 'Rome has become a Greek city,' complained the Roman writer Juvenal in the first century AD. 'Teacher, speaker, painter, trainer of wrestlers, doctor – these hungry little Greeks know everything!'

This Roman is happily checking the statue his slaves are erecting in his garden – even though his accountant, a Greek slave, is telling him how much it cost.

The statue has been brought from Greece. 'Is there one statue, one picture, that has not been captured and brought here from the places we have defeated in war?' asked the Roman politician Cicero in 70 BC.

Although the Romans have defeated the Greek armies, the Greek way of life has conquered Rome.

How Do We Know?

The Greeks did not invent writing; they borrowed letters from a script used in Syria in the Middle East. They were, however, the first civilization to have large numbers of people who could read and write. The first two Greek letters were *alpha* and *beta*, hence the word alphabet. Fortunately, the library at Alexandria collected and preserved ancient Greek literature, so historians can find out about the beliefs and opinions of the Greeks.

As well as the writings of philosophers and playwrights, hundreds of letters written by ordinary people have been preserved. From these we can learn about their families and businesses. Letters from children have also been saved. 'If you don't take me to Alexandria, I won't speak to you…I won't hold your hand…I won't eat. So there!' a boy writes to his father. 'To my respected father,' writes another. 'I pray for you daily…May you and my brothers be unharmed and successful for many years. Don't forget our pigeons.' Historians can deduce (work out) the personalities of the writers from their words.

Greek writings reveal other things of interest to the historian. Pausanias wrote the first guide book (AD 175), describing in detail the buildings and works of art in Greece.

The Greeks also invented the study of history; their word *historia* means enquiry. The first history books were local histories written for Greek colonists. Later, the Greek writer Herodotus (*c.* 484-425 BC), known as the Father of History, wrote an account of the Persian Wars: he was the first person to ask *how* and *why* the events of the past had taken place.

Thucydides (*c.* 460-399 BC) took these ideas further. He chose his sources carefully because he knew that not all sources are equally reliable: 'The poets exaggerate; storytellers would rather entertain their readers than tell the truth; even the accounts of eyewitnesses differ according to memory and their own opinions.' Most of what we know about the history of Greece (see pages 20-22, 28 and 52-57) comes directly from the writings of ancient Greek historians.

Art and Archaeology

Written sources are not the only source for the historian. Although most of the buildings of ancient Greece are in ruins, many have almost miraculously survived.

The most famous ancient Greek building is the Parthenon in Athens (see page 30). Originally the Temple of Athene, it became a Christian church in AD 450, and then a mosque in 1458. During a war in 1687, when it was being used as a gunpowder store, a shell hit the building and blew it up.

The Romans stripped Greece of many of its most beautiful sculptures. During the

eighteenth and nineteenth centuries, collectors took much of what the Romans had missed. In 1807 Lord Elgin, the British Ambassador to the Turks, bought those parts of the Parthenon frieze which had survived and shipped them to England. There is still a fierce debate about whether he 'stole' the sculptures or 'saved' them.

Recent excavations have revealed many of the artefacts of day-to-day life. In the agora in Athens, archaeologists found water clocks (see below), voting ballots from Greek courts (see page 49), and tiny bits of pottery with

names scratched on them, which had been used in ostracisms (see page 27).

In exceptional cases, archaeology supports the written record. A story about the philosopher Socrates described his visits to the house of Simon the cobbler in Athens. In the south-west corner of the agora archaeologists excavated the ruins of a house. They found hobnails, eyelets for laces, and the broken base of a cup with the name Simon on it.

No Greek paintings have survived, but we have some Roman copies, and a great deal of black and red Greek pottery. The scenes painted on the pots give us detailed information about everyday life (see page 45).

Ancient and Modern

The Greeks laid the foundations for the modern world by their achievements in politics,

philosophy, science, medicine, history, drama and architecture.

Above all, the Greeks passed down to us their ideal of *arete* – the desire, not only for success and wealth, but also for wisdom, justice and generosity. Speaking in 430 BC, at the funeral of those killed in the war with Sparta, Pericles reminded the Athenians that the men had died to save the democracy they enjoyed. 'Remember that all this was won by courage, a sense of duty and a feeling of honour,' he told the crowd. 'Take them as your model, for happiness comes from freedom, and freedom comes from courage.' We say similar things today at services of remembrance for those who have been killed while fighting for their country.

Although you cannot see Greek ideas in the same way that you can see the pyramids of Egypt or the Great Wall of China, they are, in fact, more important. Without them modern civilization would not have developed.

Far left: a bronze treaty tablet, *c.* 500 BC, showing Greek writing. Left: part of the Parthenon frieze.

Above: a party of French archaeologists excavating a *kouros* (see page 31) in AD 1894. Archaeologists have found many remains of Greek civilization, including the water clocks used at trials (above left); when the upper pot was empty, the speaker had to stop talking (see page 49).

Index